URBAN ROOSTS

Where Birds Nest in the City

BARBARA BASH

LITTLE, BROWN AND COMPANY

New York ~ Boston

To my husband, Steve, for his love of
the cityscape; and to Anne Hessey for
her incessant curiosity about the birds
that live here.

The Sierra Club, founded in 1892 by John Muir, has devoted
itself to the study and protection of the earth's scenic and
ecological resources — mountains, wetlands, woodlands, wild
shores and rivers, deserts and plains. The publishing pro-
gram of the Sierra Club offers books to the public as a non-
profit educational service in the hope that they may enlarge
the public's understanding of the Club's basic concerns. The
Sierra Club has some sixty chapters in the United States and
in Canada. For information about how you may participate
in its programs to preserve wilderness and the quality of life,
please address inquiries to Sierra Club, 730 Polk Street, San
Francisco, CA 94109.

Little, Brown and Company

Hachette Book Group USA
237 Park Avenue, New York, NY 10017
Visit our Web site at www.lb-kids.com

First Paperback Edition: September 1992

Title calligraphy by Barbara Bash

Library of Congress Cataloging-in-Publication Data

Bash, Barbara.
   Urban roosts: where birds nest in the city / Barbara Bash.
— 1st ed.
       p.   cm.
   Summary: Describes the birds that make their homes in
the heart of the city and examines how they have adjusted to
such a harsh urban environment.

   ISBN 978-0-316-08312-6 (pb)

   1. Birds — Nests — Juvenile literature.   2. Urban fauna —
Juvenile literature.   [1. Birds — Nests.   2. Urban animals.]
I. Title.
QL675.B37   1990
598.2'564 — dc20   89-70187

16   15

SC

Sierra Club Books / Little, Brown Books for Young Readers are
published by Little, Brown and Company (Inc.) in association
with Sierra Club Books.

Printed in China

Early in the morning you can hear
something rustling up on the ledge of
an old stone building. Even before the
city awakens, the birds are stirring in
their urban roosts.

All across the country, as their natural
habitats have been destroyed, birds
have moved to town. The ones that
have been able to adapt are thriving in
the heart of the city.

One familiar urban dweller is the pigeon. Long ago it was called a rock dove, because it lived in the rocky cliffs along the coast of Europe. Today it flourishes all over the United States in the nooks and crannies of our cities.

To the pigeon, the city may look like a wilderness full of high cliffs and deep canyons. The cliffs are buildings made of stone and brick and glass, and the canyons are windy avenues full of cars and people. Flying together in flocks, pigeons explore the city canyons looking for food and spots to roost.

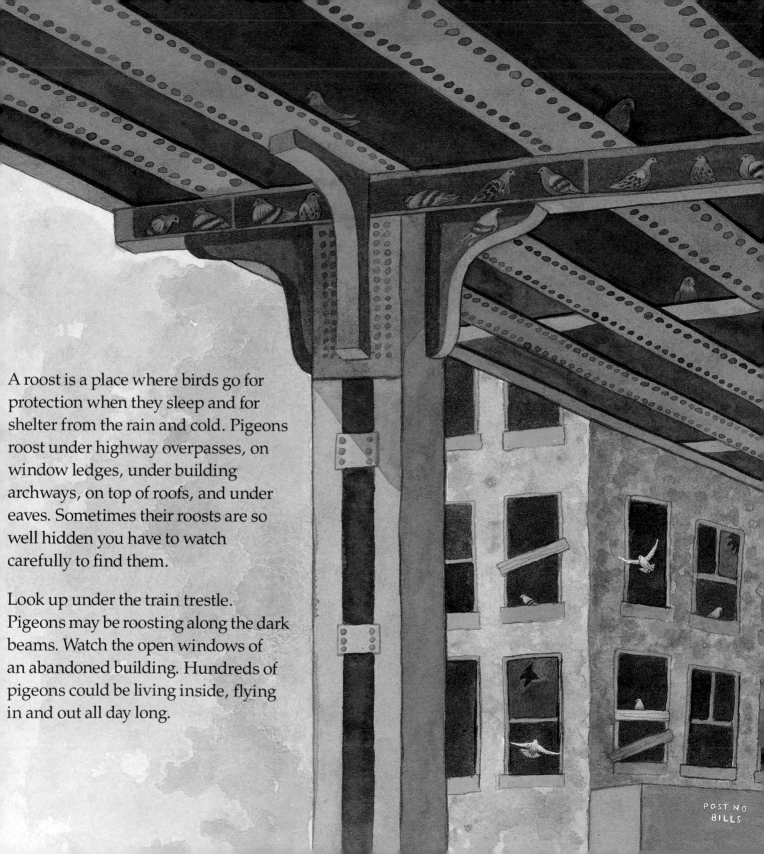

A roost is a place where birds go for protection when they sleep and for shelter from the rain and cold. Pigeons roost under highway overpasses, on window ledges, under building archways, on top of roofs, and under eaves. Sometimes their roosts are so well hidden you have to watch carefully to find them.

Look up under the train trestle. Pigeons may be roosting along the dark beams. Watch the open windows of an abandoned building. Hundreds of pigeons could be living inside, flying in and out all day long.

POST NO
BILLS

A nest is a place where birds lay their eggs and raise their chicks. Often it's in the same spot as the roost. Pigeons build a flimsy platform of sticks and twigs and debris up on a ledge, or on a windowsill, or in a flowerpot out on a fire escape, or in the curve of a storefront letter.

Throughout the year, pigeons lay eggs and hatch their young. The female sits quietly on her clutch, and after eighteen days fuzzy chicks begin to appear. Five weeks later, after their adult feathers are fully developed, the young pigeons fly away to find homes of their own.

Sparrows and finches are successful city dwellers, too. Introduced from England in 1870 to control insects, the house sparrow has chosen to live close to people all across the United States. The house finch was originally a West Coast native, but some caged birds were released on the East Coast in 1940, and the species quickly spread. Sparrows and finches don't migrate, so you can watch them at backyard feeders throughout the year, chirping and chattering as they pick up seeds.

female

HOUSE SPARROW

male

male

HOUSE FINCH

female

The little hollows in and around building ornaments and Gothic sculptures are favorite nesting spots for sparrows and finches. These cavity nesters can slip into the tiniest spaces. Some of their nests are visible and others are completely hidden from view.

In the spring, you may see a small bird flying overhead with a twig in its beak. If you follow its flight, it will lead you to its nest. Watch the bird land and then disappear into a crevice or behind a stone curve. A few moments later it will pop out again, empty-beaked, and fly away to search for more nesting material.

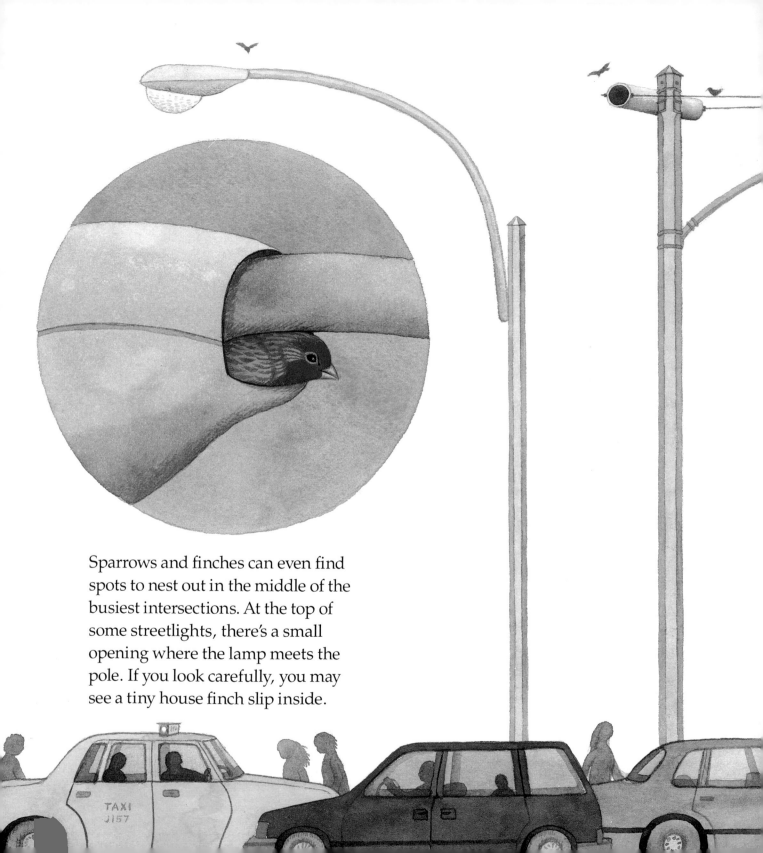

Sparrows and finches can even find spots to nest out in the middle of the busiest intersections. At the top of some streetlights, there's a small opening where the lamp meets the pole. If you look carefully, you may see a tiny house finch slip inside.

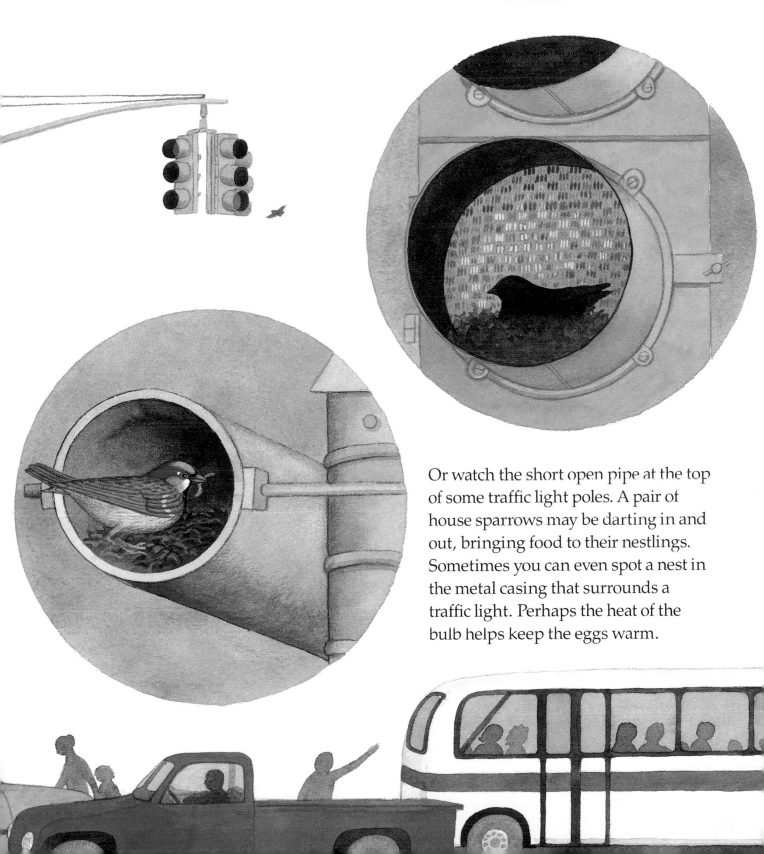

Or watch the short open pipe at the top of some traffic light poles. A pair of house sparrows may be darting in and out, bringing food to their nestlings. Sometimes you can even spot a nest in the metal casing that surrounds a traffic light. Perhaps the heat of the bulb helps keep the eggs warm.

A tiled roof can house so many
sparrows and finches it looks a little
like an apartment complex. All day
long the birds bring nesting material
and food for their chicks into the small
hidden cavities behind the tiles. When
the chicks get too big for the nest,
they play on top of the tiles, testing
their wings before their first flight.

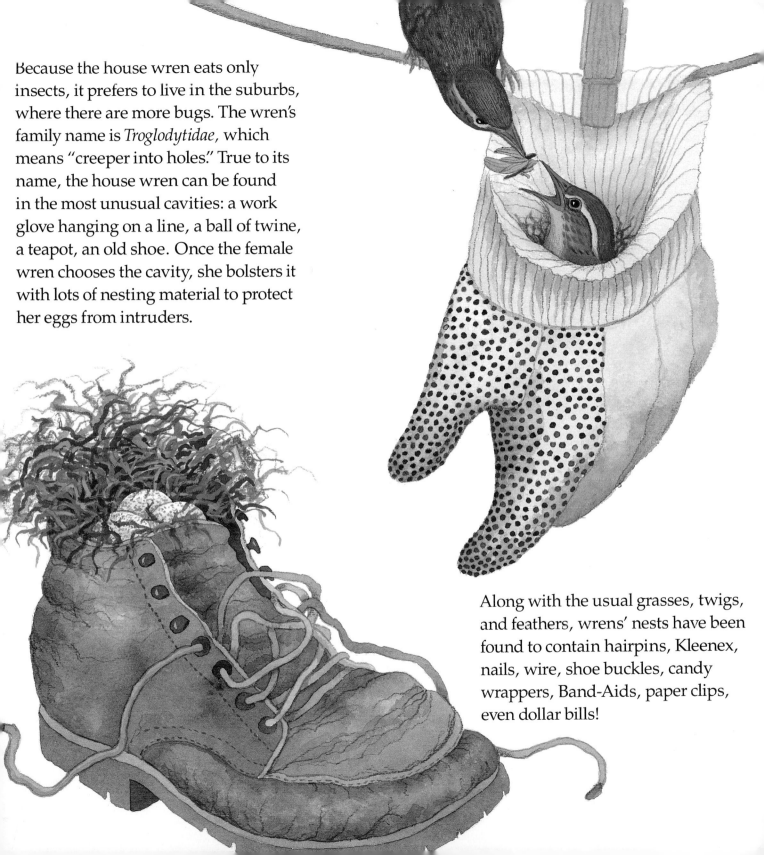

Because the house wren eats only insects, it prefers to live in the suburbs, where there are more bugs. The wren's family name is *Troglodytidae,* which means "creeper into holes." True to its name, the house wren can be found in the most unusual cavities: a work glove hanging on a line, a ball of twine, a teapot, an old shoe. Once the female wren chooses the cavity, she bolsters it with lots of nesting material to protect her eggs from intruders.

Along with the usual grasses, twigs, and feathers, wrens' nests have been found to contain hairpins, Kleenex, nails, wire, shoe buckles, candy wrappers, Band-Aids, paper clips, even dollar bills!

The barn owl lives in the city, too, but few people see it because it flies while everyone sleeps. All night long its pale, ghostly form soars over the buildings as it hunts for rats and mice to bring to its young.

The barn owl's eyes can see in the dark and its ears can hear the tiniest scratching. Even its voice is suited to city life; when it cries out in the night, it sounds like brakes screeching.

At daybreak, barn owls return to their nests to sleep. They like to live under train and highway overpasses and inside old barns and steeples. Instead of building nests, they lay their eggs in flat, protected spots. As baby barn owls grow, they huddle together, hissing and slurping, as they wait for their parents to return with food.

The nighthawk is a ground-nesting bird; it looks for a level open surface on which to lay its eggs. Because city ground is full of cars and people, the nighthawk often hatches its young up on flat graveled rooftops.

If you look up on a warm summer night, you might see a nighthawk swooping low over the streetlights, sweeping hundreds of insects into its large gaping mouth. Or you might hear its call in the dark... *peent*... *peent*....

Like the nighthawk, the killdeer makes no nest. It lays its eggs out in the open, in spots where the mottled eggshell pattern will be well camouflaged. In the city you might find killdeer eggs sitting on the gravel at the edge of a parking lot or next to a train track. Once, killdeer eggs were even found along the end line of a soccer field!

The barn swallow used to nest under the natural overhangs of cliffs. Now its nest can be found under the eaves of a house or up in the rafters of a garage. Often attached to a vertical surface, the nest is a cup made of mud and clay mixed with straw and grass, and lined with soft feathers.

In the fall, chimney swifts migrate south in groups. You might see them just before sunset as they circle around and around a large chimney, all flying in the same direction. As the sky deepens, they begin to drop inside, like a long stream of smoke being drawn back down the chimney. Inside, the swifts cluster like shingles on a roof, clinging to the sooty walls with their sharp nails.

During the winter, crows also flock together in large groups. They roost at night in the tops of trees in city parks. At dusk, one or two arrive first, perching on high branches and making a silky rustle with their wings. As the light fades, more crows appear and the clamor increases. They make rattling sounds, catlike cries, and metallic squeaks while they jostle for spots. As the darkness deepens, the calls gradually die down, until only an occasional gurgle is heard. Then the crows settle in for the night.

Starlings gather in large groups, too—often roosting all along the ledges of a building. When the winter is coldest, they crowd together in crevices to keep warm. Over a hundred starlings have been found huddled side by side in a cavity only two feet wide and three feet deep.

Winter plumage

Summer

In November, snowy owls migrate down from the arctic tundra to spend the winter in northern cities. They seem to like the windswept environment of airport landing fields—perhaps because it reminds them of home. The owls roost out on the open ground, blending in with the snowy whiteness.

At dusk the snowy owls begin hunting for mice, rats, and rabbits. They fly slowly and silently, their heads turning from side to side, their eyes scanning the ground for movement. Sometimes snowy owls will crouch on a small mound of snow and wait, completely still, for prey to wander by. The sound of the jets doesn't seem to faze them at all.

ars and trucks lumber noisily over
g city bridges. But underneath,
dden among the beams and girders,
eregrine falcons have found a home.
eekly built with powerful wings, the
lcon is one of the fastest birds on
rth. In the city it soars high above
e bridges and buildings, hunting for
geons and small birds flying below.
hen it spots its prey, the falcon folds
wings tight against its body and
ves straight down at speeds of over
e hundred fifty miles per hour!

In cities all across the country, people are fascinated with the peregrine falcon and are doing what they can to make this noble bird feel welcome. In many cities people set nesting boxes filled with gravel out on skyscraper ledges. The falcons seem to like these windy, rocky heights, for they return to the boxes early each spring to lay their eggs and raise their chicks. Living on these high perches with no natural enemies and plenty of pigeons, the falcons are adapting well to urban life.

So many birds make their homes in the
midst of the city—sparrows and
finches, barn owls and snowy owls,
swallows and swifts, nighthawks and
killdeers, pigeons and wrens, crows,
starlings, and falcons. Each has found
its own urban roost.